P9-DBS-658

TOWNSHIP OF UNION
FREE PUBLIC LIBRARY

Farm Animals

Chickens

Rachael Bell

TOWNSHIP OF UNION
FREE PUBLIC LIBRARY

Heinemann Library
Chicago, Illinois

©2000 Reed Educational & Professional Publishing
Published by Heinemann Library,
an imprint of Reed Educational & Professional Publishing,
100 N. LaSalle, Suite 1010
Chicago, IL 60602

Customer Service 888-454-2279

All rights reserved. No part of this publication may be reproduced or transmitted in any form or by any means, electronic or mechanical, including photocopying, recording, taping, or any information storage and retrieval system, without permission in writing from the publisher.

Designed by AMR
Originated by Ambassador Litho

Printed in Hong Kong/China

04 03 02 01 00
10 9 8 7 6 5 4 3 2 1

Library of Congress Cataloging-in-Publication Data
Bell, Rachael.
    Chickens / Rachael Bell.
        p. cm. – (Farm animals)
    Includes bibliographical references and index.
    Summary: Introduces the familiar farm animal, exploring birth, growth, living conditions, and uses of the chicken.
    ISBN 1-57572-530-4 (library binding)
    1. Chickens—Juvenile literature. [1. Chickens.] I. Title.
SF487.5.B45 2000
636.5—dc21
99-044494
CIP

$13.95

J
636.5
BEL
C.1

3-00

Acknowledgments
The Publishers would like to thank the following for permission to reproduce photographs: Agripicture/Peter Dean, p. 24; Anthony Blake Picture Library, pp. 21, 23; Bruce Coleman/Jane Burton, p. 5; Farmers Weekly Picture Library, p. 20; Holt Studios/Sarah Rowland, p. 4; Holt Studios/Michael Mayer, p.10; Holt Studios/Inga Spence, pp. 11, 25, 27; Holt Studios/Gordon Roberts, pp. 12, 18; Holt Studios/Bjorn Ullhagen, p. 14; Holt Studios/Richard Anthony, p. 15; Holt Studios/Nigel Cattlin, pp. 17, 28; Chris Honeywell, p. 22; Images of Nature/FLPA/Peter Dean, p. 6; Images of Nature/FLPA/Gerard Lacz, pp. 8, 9; NHPA/Joe Blossom, p. 26; Researchers Inc./Kenneth H. Thomas, p. 19; Roger Scruton, p. 29; Lynn Stone, pp. 7, 13; Tony Stone Images/Tony Page, p. 16.

Cover photograph reproduced with permission of The Stock Market.

Our thanks to the American Farm Bureau Federation for their comments in the preparation of this book.

Every effort has been made to contact copyright holders of any material reproduced in this book. Any omissions will be rectified in subsequent printings if notice is given to the Publisher.

Some words are shown in bold, **like this.** You can find out what they mean by looking in the glossary.

Contents

Chicken Relatives

Chickens are farm birds that come in many sizes and colors. There are many different kinds of chickens. People all over the world **raise** chickens.

Farm chickens are related to wild chickens that still live in the jungles of **Asia.** Wild chickens fly up into trees at night to keep out of danger.

Welcome to the Farm

On this farm there are hundreds of **free range** chickens in a grassy field. They are very friendly. When they see people, they think they are going to be fed!

Farmers often **raise** more than one kind of animal. On this farm, there are also cows.

Meet the Chickens

tail

wing

ear
(it is just
a hole)

nostril

beak

leg

The female chicken is called a hen. She
lays about six eggs at a time. Then
she sits on them for 21 days. This
keeps them warm until they **hatch.**

comb

wattle

spur

foot
(four
toes)

Male chickens are called roosters.
They are bigger than hens and have
larger **combs** and **wattles**. Their
feathers are more colorful. Roosters
may use their **spurs** to fight enemies.

Meet the Baby Chickens

Baby chickens are called chicks.
They have a special egg tooth on
their beaks to help them break their
shell when they **hatch.** Chicks are
covered in **down.**

Chicks make a cheeping sound. The hen teaches them to feed. She pecks at food, then drops it for the chicks to eat. They copy her and learn to peck.

Where Do Chickens Live?

On this farm, the chickens live in hen houses. These stand in a large field of grass. An electric fence keeps **predators** out.

Each house has a thick layer of **shavings** on the floor. This keeps the chickens' feet clean and dry. Each house has egg boxes. The farmer opens them from outside to collect the eggs.

What Do Chickens Eat?

Chickens peck at anything to see if it is
good to eat. They eat plants, seeds,
dirt, insects, and worms. Chickens
swallow their food without chewing it.
The food is ground up in the **gizzard.**

Chickens peck at the grass. They also
eat wheat and a **cereal** mix called
layers' mash from a **trough**. They
drink from a **waterer**.

Staying Healthy

Chickens have wings, but they cannot fly too far. They need plenty of space to run around. They prefer grass because it keeps their feet clean.

Chickens **preen** to keep their feathers clean. They comb them with their beaks. They also take dust baths. This helps them stay cool.

How Do Chickens Sleep?

Young chicks sleep under their mother during the day and at night. She fluffs up her feathers to let them all underneath her.

Like other birds, chickens roost at night. Their feet hold onto a branch, so they cannot fall off when they are asleep! Some hen houses have rods for chickens to roost on.

Raising Chickens

The farmer opens up the hen houses as soon as it is light. In the evening, he closes them again. He also fills up the food and water.

It is a lot of work to **raise** hens, so this farmer buys his hens from someone else. He buys them at four months old, just before they start **laying** eggs.

How Are Chickens Used?

Chickens are **raised** for the eggs they **lay**. A hen can lay more than two hundred eggs in one year! Eggs can be cooked in many ways. Eggs are also used in making foods such as cakes and bread.

Chickens called **roasters** or **broilers** are raised for their meat. There are lots of ways to cook chicken.

Other Chicken Farms

Some big chicken farms sell thousands of eggs. On these farms, the hens stay inside. The eggs are collected every day. They are cleaned and sold to stores.

Most of the chicken meat we buy comes from big farms that only **raise broilers**. These chickens grow big very quickly.

More Chicken Farms

Some farms **raise** many different types of chickens. Some farmers like to raise brightly colored or **bantam** chickens. They may show them at fairs.

Some special farms called hatcheries
raise chicks to sell to other farmers.
These farms often use machines to
incubate the eggs.

Fact File

Chickens do not have a good sense of taste or smell. But chickens can see and hear very well.

They can learn to do simple tricks if someone **rewards** them with food.

Chickens have special **organs** in their legs that can feel tiny **vibrations** in the ground. They can feel any enemy coming toward them long before they can see them.

The heaviest type of chicken in the world is called the White Sully. The largest of these was a rooster named Weirdo. In 1973, Weirdo weighed 22 pounds (10 kilograms)—that's as much as a small dog!

Chickens have a special pouch in their throats called a crop. The

crop holds the food and then sends it to the stomach.

Glossary

Asia largest land area of the world that includes countries such as China, Vietnam, and Thailand

bantam very small type of chicken

broiler chicken that is ready to eat at five to twelve weeks of age

cereal wheat, oats, and barley, often made into breakfast food or feed for animals

comb skin flap on top of a chicken's head

down small, soft, fluffy feathers that cover a chick's body

free range animals that are mostly kept outside and have plenty of space

gizzard muscular part of a chicken's stomach that helps grind food

hatch to come out of an egg

incubate to keep eggs warm so that they hatch

lay when an egg comes out of a female chicken

layers' mash special food for laying hens made of mixed cereals.

nostril opening in the body that lets air in

organ special part of the body

predator animal that kills another animal for food

preen to clean by gripping a feather and pulling down with the beak

raise to bring up young animals or children

reward to give food in return for doing something well

roaster chicken that is ready to eat when it is four to six months old

shaving tiny piece of wood that is soft and fluffy

spur bony part that sticks out of a male chicken's leg

trough long, open container that holds food for animals

vibration tiny, fast movement that can sometimes be felt from a distance

waterer type of water fountain for animals

wattle flap of skin that hangs from the chin of a chicken

More Books to Read

Brady, Peter. *Chickens.* Danbury, Conn.: Children's Press, 1996.

Hansen, Ann L. *Chickens.* Minneapolis: ABDO Publishing Company, 1998.

Kallen, Stuart A. *The Farm.* Minneapolis: ABDO Publishing Company, 1997.

Royston, Angela. *Chicken.* Des Plaines, Ill.: Heinemann Library, 1998.

Stone, Lynn M. *Chickens.* Vero Beach, Fla. : Rourke Corporation, 1990.

Index

FREE PUBLIC LIBRARY UNION, NEW JERSEY

3 9549 00373 6347

TOWNSHIP OF UNION
FREE PUBLIC LIBRARY

AAW- 4258